The Unwritten Rules of Professional Etiquette

The Unwritten Rules of Professional Etiquette

Building a Positive Reputation in Graduate School

Ryan Sharma

Habile Press

Published in the United States of America
First Edition, July 2020
ISBN-13: 978-1-7349805-0-9

Library of Congress Control Number: 2020907790

Habile Press
1280 S. Victoria Ave, #230
Ventura, CA 93003

Editing by Ed Levy
Cover design by BookBaby

For Ethan, Eliana, and Henry

ACKNOWLEDGMENTS

I would like to thank the many people who supported and encouraged my effort to bring this book to life. To my loving wife, Susan, whose confidence in me has always made me think bigger. I am particularly grateful to Jamie Bedics and Ron Bale for their many thoughtful and honest comments on earlier drafts. I also appreciate Lauren Mills and Lori Selby for early reviews and feedback. Thank you to Shawn Smith, whose advice has been both incredibly supportive and invaluable. Thank you, also, to my editor, Ed Levy, for his hard work in finalizing the manuscript. I am extremely grateful to my lifelong friend, Rob Malesko, for his help proofreading the final draft.

Importantly, thank you to all my teachers who took the time and effort to shape the best in me. Thank you to my students, particularly those who always challenged me to be reflective, more human, and a better professional. To all the students who showed me that even the most difficult professional challenges can lead to profound personal growth, your dedication and self-honesty are inspiring.

CONTENTS

Introduction

Every student enters graduate school with many forms of debt. The most obvious is financial, but your debt is also in the knowledge, awareness, and skills relevant to your discipline. The faculty are there to bring you up to their professional level; they have already endured years of education, training, licensure, and practice—all of which they offer to you as you prepare for the same path. A professional attitude is one that accepts their work on your behalf by opening yourself to this offering. It communicates that you value the time and effort that they devote to your preparation, dedicate yourself to the training, and honor the professional community and its image.

I care greatly about my students and their ultimate success, which is why I hold such a high bar for them while they are under my training. I have noticed that I intermittently tuck advice inside the manuals I write, the emails I send, and the lectures I give. I have decided to share that advice in this book so that you, too, can maximize your success. If I can lift you up with some of the suggestions in this book, then it elevates us all.

The purpose of this book is twofold. First, it provides you with situational awareness of how faculty members are most likely to judge professional etiquette. Second, it provides concrete, immediately applicable advice on appropriate professional responses to those situations you are likely to encounter. I am writing down many of the unwritten rules. I will also share with you why those rules exist so that you may have a successful graduate-level academic experience and future professional life.

Although this book was motivated by the experiences and the values that I believe are most relevant to professional deportment, I have focused on widely shared expectations gathered from other professors, ethical case studies, and broad psychological principles. I believe these expectations are similar to ones found in other disciplines and areas of study and can effectively serve as a starting point as you evaluate your own behaviors in your program.

Here is my first piece of advice: Seek out a mentor who can help you navigate the professional path. A mentor is someone you trust to understand your context and give sound advice. Students often approach me for guidance on how best to respond to a challenging situation. Seeking such advice is not only appropriate but also a sign of strength.

A Note on Terms

The people in your program who have evaluative power or authority are the ones who will most directly judge your professionalism. Because of this, I use terms such as *professor*, *faculty member*, *instructor*, *supervisor*, and *advisor* somewhat interchangeably; teaching assistants and other senior students may also at times fill teaching or advising roles. It cannot be overstated that how you behave around staff as well as peers also shapes your professional reputation. For example, when a student is rude to our administrative assistant, the faculty hears about it. When students come forward with a concern about the behavior of one of their peers, the faculty will investigate. All of this protects the profession.

So, apply the rules of professional etiquette to everyone around you—no exceptions.

CHAPTER 1

Why Professionalism Matters

Have you ever worked with or hired someone, found that they did high-quality work and were very competent, but you really disliked working with them? Maybe you knew a teacher who was exceptionally knowledgeable but also unreliable, aloof, or critical. Perhaps you hired a personal trainer who created excellent routines for you but was frequently unavailable, did not communicate with you, or did not follow through on agreements. What was it like working with them? How did you describe these people to others? How have others described these kinds of professionals to you? Conversely, have you ever hired someone who fell short on their work but did their best to meet your needs? Perhaps someone lost your important paperwork but apologized and helped expedite a new set of forms. What about the therapist or physician who was unable to help you with your condition but made sure to connect you to someone who could?

Examples like these highlight the clear difference between competence and professionalism. Your work quality and your interpersonal skills and attitude are distinctly different areas of development. You can be very competent in your work—doing everything with high quality—and yet be difficult to work with. You can be competent and unprofessional or incompetent and professional. You could also be both competent and professional, though you could also be neither.

The distinction between competence and professionalism is the reason you cannot assume that, just because you show up to classes in graduate school and get good grades, you will have everything you need to carry you through your career. This misunderstanding is likely fueled by the perception that grades are everything, which is what you may have learned as an undergrad. Unfortunately, grades only measure your competence in the subject matter and not your professionalism. After all, acting professionally is not required when learning statistics, for example—you could learn those math skills quite efficiently while also being rude.

Even more complicated, the application of professionalism to specific situations varies not only by profession but also by context. For example, the particular expectations of a lawyer may be different from those of a teacher, and what may work in a hospital might not work in a business office. In both cases, the would-be professional will have to make a judgment based on the best available options. The fact that professionalism requires judgment necessarily means that there is no single "right" way to be professional in every situation. That is why you need to develop a mindset that maintains focus on your professional responsibilities.

Professional Development in Your Program

Because it is difficult to define professionalism in an exhaustive way for every situation, some programs may not have venues for teaching it directly. Does your program give you a course in professional development? Are you referred to any books on the topic? Do you have structured mentoring in professionalism? Most of the time, your training in professionalism happens informally through your ongoing interactions with faculty who are willing to guide you through these unwritten rules. Each email reply, comment, and directive that you get from faculty are mini-lessons for the way to go about things as a professional.

If you take notice of this training, the conglomeration of these experiences will begin to coalesce around the subtle expectations of professional etiquette. If you do not notice this training, you may feel lost in a sea of expectations that you do not understand. Sure, there are general principles that guide professional attitude and deportment, but how do you apply those principles when excusing yourself from class, for example? You may have intended to be congenial when you emailed the professor about missing class, but maybe you did not anticipate the professor noticing that, in your disregard for classroom participation expectations, you violated a professional code of responsibility and accountability.

Your graduate faculty is interested in developing your professionalism for many reasons, but two of the most immediate are important to mention here. First, being professional increases your success, and most faculty are genuinely interested in your success. Having a highly tuned and professional skillset makes you a better manager, physician, or lawyer. Second, student professionalism directly affects the program's reputation. Whether it is during their enrollment in the program or after graduation, a student's conduct and reputation in the larger community necessarily reflect back on the school. When my students embark on their clinical training placements, I tell them explicitly that they are to always think of themselves as ambassadors of our university. As a student in your program, you will also carry the name of your school with you when you are in networking meetings, conferences, or workgroups with others. Your success in these contexts is also your program's success.

There is also something much larger at play here because your program exists in a community of other graduate programs with the same goal of preparing students for the profession, and that community in turn exists within the greater professional community. At each of these levels, there is a recognition of shared goals with something larger, and this is the essence of developing a professional identity and professional values: *When you realize that your words and conduct are part of something much larger than yourself, you begin to see yourself as the embodiment of your profession.* Having this perspective prompts you to consider how others experience not only you but also your profession through your behaviors.

Your faculty's shared interests with the larger training community and the profession underscore their motivation in developing your professionalism. Your graduate program is a microcosm of society, and as such, it functions as the perfect practice environment for building this perspectival shift. Your faculty is your front line for such practice.

The Consequences of Professionalism

Your professional reputation carries influence that leads to both tangible and intangible effects. How your faculty experience you personally is necessarily part of their impression of you globally, and that global impression influences faculty behavior whether or not it is conscious, positive, or fair. Human beings are naturally social creatures, and our social interactions are the fabric of our realities. When you experience a wrinkle in that fabric, you notice. Conversely, when you experience a silky smoothness in that fabric, you also notice.

The psychological principle working here is called the *halo effect*. Basically, it describes the tendency for positive or negative impressions in one domain to bleed over into other domains. For example, if I experience a student in class as highly responsible and intelligent, I may assume that they would also be a great research assistant even when I have no information about their ability to fill that role. Conversely, if a student is perpetually late with assignments in class, I may assume that their time management difficulties could get in the way of performing adequately in a clinical placement.

Think about all the individuals with whom you interact on a daily basis, be they restaurant servers, doctors, bank tellers, computer repair specialists, sales associates, administrative assistants, mechanics, insurance agents, and so on. Each of these encounters consists of many micro-events that leave us with an impression of their professionalism. Did they greet you with a smile? Did they listen to your concerns and understand your needs? Or did they seem to be doing something else while trying to help you, like answering an email or texting a friend? Did they give you faulty information and then deny it was their fault? That impression will probably influence whether or not you want to approach them again.

Now think about the impact of transmitting that person's reputation to others who may not have had any direct experience with them. For example, imagine that you need an eye exam and you ask a friend about the optometrist that they just saw. Your friend—whose opinion you trust—describes her as "very professional" and generally enjoyed the experience. Consider the following questions:

- Do you think you will make an appointment with her?

- Do you get a sense that she will probably meet your expectations?

- Would you trust her judgment?

- If, for whatever reason, she advertised a position you could apply for, would you look into it?

- If, for whatever reason, you were in a position to hire an optometrist, would you ask her to apply?

Now imagine that you had to make an appointment with a different optometrist whom your friend describes as "unprofessional." Consider the following questions:

- How do you feel about having to deal with him in a formal capacity?

- Do you worry about trusting his work or making special requests?

- Do you want to give him your money?

- If, for whatever reason, he advertised a position you could apply for, would you look into it?

- If for whatever reason you were in a position to hire an optometrist, would you ask him to apply?

This thought experiment highlights how a professional

reputation shapes the assumptions, emotions, and behaviors of others. It has real consequences whether we experience it ourselves or are told so by others: We are drawn toward those who are professional and are repelled by those who are unprofessional, even if they might be very competent in their job.

How you behave around your faculty will create the same kinds of assumptions, emotions, and behaviors in them. Do you want your faculty to be drawn to you? Or do you want to become the student whose name prompts heavy sighs and eye rolls behind closed doors? *Get the halo effect working in your favor.* Being a student whom faculty feel drawn to has clear benefits, including:

1. *Access to opportunities.* Perhaps the most tangible impact of a positive impression is gaining access to opportunities. At any given time, faculty may be looking for teaching assistants, graduate assistants, research assistants, supervisees, or mentees to work with them on special projects. If these opportunities are of interest to you, then you need to be the kind of student whom the faculty wants to work with. Being smart about the project or having a lot of interest in it is helpful, but are you also dependable, responsive, and open to feedback? In most cases, I prefer students with stronger professional skills over those with more competence because they will be easier to work with.

2. *Professional recommendations.* The way in which you are experienced necessarily colors the manner in which your professors provide your professional recommendations, whether in a letter of recommendation or as a reference for a job application. At my university, half

the questions on our faculty reference checks are about competence and half are about professionalism (such as collegiality, dependability, and flexibility), which highlights the importance of these professional qualities. In letters of recommendation, the difference between a good and a great recommendation is subtle but noticeable to other readers. Great recommendations may include more adjectives, a positive comparison of the student to the referee's other students, or assurances that the student comes with their highest recommendation.

3. *Standing out in a crowded field.* How do you stand out among your peers when everyone is taking the same classes, getting the same grades, and doing the same extracurricular activities? Few students realize that there is significant grade inflation in graduate school and that everyone is in the same process of padding their resumes and vitaes with extra volunteer activities. While these aspects of your performance are important, your professional reputation will be what sets you apart. I can think of many students who did well in our program, but I remember most fondly those who excelled in professional deportment.

Being the kind of student faculty want to work with is no different than being the kind of applicant employers want to hire. Some students mistakenly think they can just wait until they graduate to start acting professionally, not realizing that (a) their reputation is preceding them and (b) they have missed out on the practice of meeting expectations.

CHAPTER 2

Learning the Expectations

Just because some of the rules of professional etiquette are unwritten does not mean that you have to learn them the hard way by bumping through your program and making mistakes. There are several ways to deduce the general principles that embody your profession's identity. When you know these general principles, you can determine how those expectations should manifest in certain situations. Professors refer to this as one's *professional attitude*. It means that you bring a professional mindset to every professional situation. That mindset is built from these general principles.

Flexibility and adaptability are essential skills that facilitate learning to apply broad principles to specific situations. Sometimes it will take trial and error, and sometimes you may have different faculty members with different expectations. Your ability to adapt quickly will be noticed. Faculty know that developing a professional attitude takes time and practice, and your sincere interest in wanting to will be respected and valued.

Aside from reading books like this one, there are several concrete strategies for building a professional attitude that do not come from the school of hard knocks.

1. Search the Existing Materials

Professors may be upfront with their expectations and write them out explicitly in their syllabi, handbooks, manuals, or training agreements. If you do not read these carefully, you may miss important information about expectations. Notice what is being said. Is there a paragraph about late paperwork? Is there a full page about professional dress? Are they using strong language or boldface font anywhere? Are the policies around tardiness and absences inflexible?

Take note of these details: Your professors are telling you in advance the issues with students that they are hoping to avoid. If students using their cell phones in my class create a problem, you had better believe that my next syllabus will include a policy on cell phone use. If you do not read this in the syllabus and violate this policy, you join the cadre of students whom I regard as disrespectful and unprofessional.

The same goes for the student handbook, which is generally considered the voice of all faculty in the program. When we need to establish new guidelines regarding behaviors we want to encourage in our students, we create a new section in the handbook. It behooves you to learn these guidelines in advance. You may also want to note the section on "Student Rights and Responsibilities." In addition to stating the rights that you have as a student, they also articulate the values that the program or university sees as integral to your effective participation in the educational process.

2. Know the Ethics in Your Profession

There are national organizations representing the interests of almost any kind of profession that you can think of.

Whether you are a nurse, physician, dentist, spa or salon owner, accountant, lawyer, business manager, counselor, teacher, or heating and cooling contractor, there is a national association that works on behalf of your interests. These associations are often involved in advocacy, education, public policy, and workforce development—all activities that promote and shape the profession as it adjusts to the needs and demands of the public. In addition to these important activities, professional organizations publish ethical codes or standards of conduct for their members. Sometimes called *Principles and Code of Ethics, Best Practices,* or *Code of Conduct,* these documents are frequently revised and ratified by the membership and reflect the professional characteristics desired of those operating under the auspices of that profession. As public documents, they serve as proclamations of self-described principles and character traits. Most important in these documents are the introductory chapters for "Principles" or "Preamble," which will describe the attitudes essential for effectively delivering professional services.

Your graduate faculty members have already gone through the process of learning and developing their own professional identity that reflects these ethical codes. As such, those same principles become yardsticks by which you are measured in the program. I recommend that you find and read the code of ethics that most closely relates to your field of study.

3. Use the Power of Observation

You can also learn a lot about a professor's values and expectations by being attentive and observant because they leak their values through their intermittent comments and behaviors. Some faculty may frequently cite maxims or adages, which are short phrases or sentences that capture large ideas and values. A supervisor who says, "Smooth seas do not make skillful sailors" is expecting you to embrace difficulty. They may also selectively compliment or reprimand certain student behavior. If you happen to notice a reprimand happening to another student instead of yourself, all the better.

As an example of reading behaviors, I once had to attend group supervision after class at my supervisor's office off-campus. Because there was a sizable break between supervision and the preceding class, I sometimes used that time to run errands. One day, when I did not have any errands, I was so early that I sat in his waiting room and read several articles that I had brought with me. He saw me in passing, smiled brightly, and complimented me for preparing and being ready for supervision. On another day, when I had to run some errands after class and was close to being late, I happened to walk briskly off the elevator and through his office door as he was closing it to start supervision. The message on his face as I passed him was unmistakable: *You're lucky.* This supervisor clearly had high expectations around both preparedness and timeliness.

4. Know the Values that are Universal

There are many values that are so universally revered as hallmarks of professionalism that they transcend disciplines. Some of them might be considered baseline standards while others may be truly aspirational, requiring continuous practice and refinement over the course of a career.

PREPAREDNESS

I once had an appointment with my primary care physician, and she walked in the door with my chart, opened it, and said, "Okay, so who do we have today?" While she is a very competent physician, what she communicated to me at that moment was that I was just another person in line at her office. Apparently, I was not worth any extra effort or preparation on her part, and she was planning on dealing with my issues on the fly. While it is very possible she could do so competently, it felt very unprofessional to me. The net result was that I did not think she was truly interested in my concerns. I felt disposable.

Being prepared shows your seriousness about the work that you do and the people it affects. The graduate faculty expects the same kind of seriousness in your training. Being prepared in graduate school means taking ownership of your education and not expecting your faculty to do it for you. This extends far beyond classroom participation. For example, situations in which it is important to be mindful of being prepared are recurring meetings with your dissertation or thesis advisor, clinical supervision, your work as a graduate or teaching assistant, and special projects with faculty (for example, helping with program evaluation, representing the student council, or managing research programs). Following are some common ways to demonstrate preparation in these contexts:

- *Have your tasks completed.* Usually, between meetings certain tasks will be expected of you. For example, if you agreed to add at least five pages to your literature review at your last meeting with your dissertation advisor, make sure you have it done.

- *Attempt to first answer your questions yourself.* This is relevant if your question is with a policy or another program responsibility. It is very annoying having to spend time explaining something that is already explained elsewhere. It is the reason why we write handbooks. For instance, if you have a question about when you are eligible to walk in the graduation ceremony, you should first look for the answer in your program's handbook or catalog. Similarly, if you have a question about the methodology for your thesis, attempt to find the answer in the class materials from your methods course.

- *Have questions ready ahead of time.* If you show up to a meeting or appointment without questions, it comes off as passive and sends the message that you want the other person to do the thinking and work for you. If you are lost on a project and do not know how to move forward, have an idea of where you ultimately want to get to so that the advisor can be more useful. Write down your questions and ideas if necessary. In clinical supervision, showing up without questions communicates to your supervisor that you already know everything and do not have anything to improve on. This does not spark confidence in a supervisor.

- *Help the faculty help you.* Let them know what kind of support is most helpful or needed at the time. If you want help brainstorming ideas for how to address a problem, let them know. If you would rather receive concrete direction, ask if this is okay. If you are just looking to get an opinion on how to move forward in a unique situation, communicate that you already have an idea of what to do.

- *Take notes.* Get concrete directions for next time and follow them.

- *Say, "Thank you."*

RESPONSIBILITY

Taking ownership and being accountable for both your learning and your learning environment is the hallmark of responsibility. Responsible students are open to feedback, work hard to make changes, and approach difficult situations when needed. Irresponsible students blame others for their difficulties, make excuses, and avoid challenging situations or leave them for others to manage.

RELIABILITY

When I experience a student as reliable and dependable, I feel a sense of ease and comfort around them. I can trust that they will do something when asked. Even if what they do is not high quality (not fully competent), I still trust that they will work hard and learn and that the next time I ask them to do something they will do it.

INTEGRITY

Integrity means doing what you say and saying what is true. Integrity also means being principled, consistent, and undivided. It is perhaps the hardest professional characteristic to actualize because it requires that a professional attitude and identity permeate your entire being.

HONESTY

One of the most concerning behaviors for me as a faculty member is observing students being untruthful or dishonest. Common examples include the unauthorized use of other sources (plagiarism), lying, cheating, or making excuses to avoid consequences. While this may have worked for you in undergrad, do not attempt to use dishonesty in graduate school. If your trustworthiness falters, everything else will also begin to crumble away. Someone who is untrustworthy cannot also be responsible or reliable, nor can they have integrity. Being formally evaluated sometimes makes being honest difficult. How can you be honest about mistakes when the faculty are grading your competence? It may sound counterintuitive, but I see a student's willingness to be honest and vulnerable as a sign of true professionalism because it is required for accurate self-assessment. Without accurate self-assessment, we cannot grow. I do not expect students to be perfect; I expect them to be capable of growth.

5. Asking

Depending on the nature of your relationship with the faculty member, you may have the opportunity to open a conversation about expectations and requirements. This is especially true when you have a sustained working relationship with a faculty member, such as a clinical supervisor or dissertation chair. Opening this conversation may seem intimidating, but with the right attitude, it can communicate your sincere interest in getting the most out of what they can offer you. Direct questioning, such as, "What are your expectations around due dates?" may work well, but an indirect yet equally effective way to learn about a professor's values is asking what they believe makes a successful professional in your field. If you were to ask me "What separates a good psychologist from a great psychologist?" you can be sure that included among the specific skillsets (what makes one competent) that I mention you will hear a number of larger values and attitudes (what makes one professional) that permeate the work. I will tell you that a great psychologist develops skills in fostering a strong therapeutic alliance, working clients through resistance to change, and measuring the success of the treatment using behavioral outcomes. I will also tell you that a great psychologist is accountable, responsive, and honest, all qualities that I would expect students working under me to demonstrate.

Sample Questions for Starting the Conversation

What kinds of skills and characteristics will be most challenged in this opportunity?

What should I learn that is not taught in the books?

What was the hardest lesson in your own training?

Lastly, it is possible that faculty will not talk about professional expectations or may not even tell you when they see you behaving unprofessionally. Unfortunately, some faculty members will simply write you a poor evaluation or talk about your shortcomings to other faculty or in your letter of recommendation. This describes faculty who may be conflict-avoidant or otherwise uncomfortable providing constructive feedback. While you cannot control this reality, be confident in Strategies 1–4.

CHAPTER 3

How to Appropriately Miss a Class or Meeting

The catalyst for writing this chapter came from this email that I received from a student an hour before class:

Dr. Sharma,

I am feeling ill and have decided to stay home today. See you next week.

—Student

I do not have a problem with students missing classes because of illness. Instead, what bothered me most in this email is the complete disregard of any wider impacts or responsibilities. Read on its own, it appears as though the student was stating that he alone has the authority to decide whether or not the class is important. While this may not have been the intent, it was indeed the impact.

All of us learned in undergraduate training that you are responsible for your own education and that if you miss a class it is on you. In graduate school (and especially in doctoral programs), expectations are much higher than this. Your attendance is expected because it affects your peers, your instructors, your supervisors, and your clients. For example, missing a lecture on psychological treatments for depression may have the following impacts:

- The instructor may have prepared class activities that were dependent on a specific number of participants.

- Your classmates will not have the opportunity to hear your perspectives and questions during class.

- Your clients struggling with depression might receive a lower quality of care because you missed a lecture on these treatments.

- Your supervisor is responsible for those clients under your care who may not be getting the treatments that they need because you missed the class when they were taught.

If you need to excuse yourself from a class, meeting, or conference, at the very least, this should be communicated as soon as possible and include an apology for any inconvenience it may cause. I often get an email from a student the morning of class informing me of their illness, and I find this acceptable. Above and beyond the apology, it is very helpful to demonstrate to the person or persons that you recognize how your absence affects them. Thus, a statement that tempers these impacts is appropriate. Here are some essential points to include in your communication:

- An apology for the inconvenience

- Recognition of how your absence will impact everyone else

- An assumption of responsibility for anything that happens in your absence, including any assignments that were due that day or completed in class

- Some proactivity on your part, which does not necessarily rely on the instructor, to make up any work for the absence

Here is an example of a professional email excusing yourself from class:

Hi Dr. Garcia,

I'm very sorry to be missing class today. I understand that I will not be able to participate in the group presentations and will miss the content being presented by my peers. I will follow up with my classmates in getting the notes and handouts and direct any questions, feedback, or comments directly to them. Please let me know if you'd like me to do anything further or if there were any assignments completed during class that I can make up.

You do not necessarily need to include an excuse for your absence, though providing a little information can help the instructor understand and empathize. For example, if the reason is private, you can simply state that you are struggling with a "personal issue" or a "family emergency." I do not require students to submit proof of illness, though other schools, programs, or faculty may have different requirements. Be sure that you know and follow those policies.

If you happen to know that you will miss a class period in advance, it is best to ask for permission to miss the class. Do not assume that you are entitled to absences because you planned on attending a wedding, concert, or family vacation. Also, do not assume that the instructor owes you any extra time or advising because of your absence, though you may request it if needed. For example, do not assume that the instructor will give you your own private lecture on the content that you missed.

CHAPTER 4

When You Should Say Thank You

You may find it surprising that I am writing a chapter on this topic, but it is amazing how often faculty express to me their dismay at a student who did not thank them for something. Faculty have many responsibilities that go beyond working with students, and all of them are included in their evaluation by the university. For example, in addition to being evaluated on teaching and advising, we are also evaluated on our service to the university (serving on university committees), our scholarship (professional publications and presentations, grant writing), our service to the profession (volunteering and activism in professional organizations), and our service to the community (responding to community needs and developing partnerships). When a student makes a special request or needs something in the midst of these taxing demands, faculty members must renegotiate their schedules to accommodate them. While we are happy to do so, a little gratitude is always appreciated.

Whether you send a physical note, a thank-you email, or simply give a verbal "thank you" depends on the situation.

In most cases, an email is just fine and is not regarded as less appropriate than a note or card. Also, in most cases, the thank-you need not be extensive or prolonged, lest it cross the line into brown-nosing. A simple gesture of appreciation for the faculty member's time and effort is enough.

Here are some situations where some gratitude would be appropriate:

- When someone writes a letter of recommendation for you

- When someone reads your thesis or dissertation and provides feedback

- When someone answers a question for you or directs you to resources that you asked for

- After a lecture, seminar, supervision session, or group conference

- When someone provides you with a special opportunity or individual instruction

- When someone completes a form for you or helps you administratively with a program or university requirement

- When someone helps you solve a problem or when faculty members or advisors need to get involved in an issue at one of your external placements

- At the end of an interview process, to all individuals who took the time to interview you

- When someone compliments your professionalism, achievements, or effort

Special Situations

In situations where your training with someone extends beyond a typical class or semester, you should be more thoughtful with conveying your appreciation. Examples include thanking dissertation chairs who help you over the course of several years, supervisors who work with you individually through a specialized training track, or mentors who you were able to utilize for problems throughout your time in the program and afterward. If you feel that these individuals sincerely invested themselves in your growth, a more heartfelt thank-you would be appropriate. It might be most meaningful to communicate your gratitude in person, being specific about what aspects of the training or qualities of the mentor you most appreciate. If you feel shy about doing so in person, do so in a card. Do not feel compelled to include a gift unless it is an important aspect of your culture. If you do so, keep the monetary value of the gift nominal (less than $25).

CHAPTER 5

Emailing

Email is the primary form of communication in all schools and universities. While there have been many developments in communication since the advent of email, there is little reason to believe that it will soon be supplanted by other means.

There does exist a formality to email communication, which faculty use to various degrees. Some are okay with typing messages that might sound like a conversation, while others prefer that your emails look and sound more like letters. I advise that you err on the side of formality until you are sure that your faculty are okay with less formal communication; I have a colleague who regularly scolds students for lazy email habits such as sending attachments without an email body and not using salutations. Here are some points to keep in mind when composing emails to faculty:

1. *Make a descriptive subject line.* The subject line should accurately describe the purpose of your email in as few words as possible. This allows the recipient to effectively plan how to manage your email among others. I have a student who never writes a subject line, and I have to submit to being surprised when I open her emails.

2. *Use a salutation.* Some students just start typing out their message in the email body as if they were in the middle of a conversation. Don't do this. Formally address the recipient. If it is someone you interact with regularly or someone with whom you are familiar, use "Hi" and their name. If you are sending it to someone you do not know personally, use "Dear." Do not type only "Dr. Chu" as the salutation, as this sounds as though you are just calling their name. Use a comma after the salutation, not a colon.

3. *Open with a pleasantry.* Briefly make a statement that acknowledges your good intentions for the recipient. Examples include, "I hope this message finds you well," or "I hope you had a nice weekend." Note that in ongoing email threads or chains, you do not do this after the first message.

4. *Type the body of the email message.*

5. *Sign-off.* Use a sign-off appropriate to the nature of the email. If it is a simple communication, you can end with "Thanks" or "Best." If you are inviting a review of some sort (such as a thesis), use something like "I appreciate your time in reviewing my work." If you are awaiting a response to a question, you can say "I appreciate your help" or "I look forward to hearing from you."

6. *Name or Signature.* If using a signature that includes more than your name, be sure that the content is accurate and professional. While many people like to use quotes from famous people in their signature lines, it

is not really the place to be making statements or expressing platitudes.

Some Other Important Points About Email

- *Sending attachments.* Always type an email when you are just sending an attachment, even if the attachment is something the professor is expecting. If you do not, the professor needs to open the document and read it to figure out what it is and what to do with it.

- *Email name.* Most if not all email programs have an option that allows you to decide how you want your name to appear in the recipient's inbox. Enter your first and last name here without any additional credentials or words. When I was in graduate school, I thought it was funny and cute to have "Ryan the Great" as my email name, until I was rightfully instructed to change it. Some students confuse this field with the name for the email account and enter "school" or "UCLA," which is what then shows up to the confused recipient.

- *Email address.* When not using a school-issued email address, use one with some version of your name. Do not use the "crazycowgirl24" email address that you created in high school.

- *Blind carbon copy, or "bcc."* The *bcc* line in an email to Recipient 1 copies the message to Recipient 2 without Recipient 1 being aware of it. There are very few situations when this would be appropriate because, at best, it is sneaky and dishonest, especially when you know that Recipient 1 would not appreciate the message being shared without their knowledge. You are essentially drawing someone else into eavesdropping, which can make for some awkward situations and undermines transparency, trust, and integrity.

The situation where you absolutely *should* be using *bcc*? Mass emails, announcements, or newsletters. While there are probably going to be few situations where you are sending mass emails, using the *bcc* line in that situation (1) protects the privacy of each recipient, (2) prevents their email addresses from being misused by marketers or others with nefarious intent, and (3) does not let the announcement turn into a long thread of replies every time someone selects "Reply All."

- *Know when to delay responding.* If you receive an email that makes you angry, embarrassed, hurt, upset, or scared or triggers any other strong emotion, do not reply right away. Usually, your first instinct is to retort and defend yourself, but this often makes things worse. As long as the issue is not urgent, delay your response until you have had sufficient time to (1) reflect on why you reacted so strongly, and (2) have come up with a constructive response—if you are going to respond at all.

- *Check your email regularly and respond.* The best practice is to check your email daily during the week. If you agreed to use your email for contact during urgent situations, then you should also be checking on the weekends. It is appropriate to set boundaries around email use when you are on vacation, and in such instances, you should use your "Out of Office" notification system to inform senders when you will next be available to respond. If the email is also used for any kind of work function (for example, if you work as an intern, research coordinator, or teaching assistant), then you also need to include the names and contact information of persons who are covering your responsibilities while you are away.

- *Read the entire email.* This should go without saying, but you would be surprised how often I have to send a follow-up email repeating a question because the student responded to only one part of my email.

- *Address the recipient professionally.* Even as a professor and board-certified psychologist, I will address emails formally using Dr., Mr., or Ms. and the surname until I am invited to use first names. Be attentive to spelling; there is no excuse for misspelling the recipient's name when it is right there in the email.

- *Be cautious with tone.* Remember that tone is often read into written text when there is no one there to speak it. To avoid this, use polite words and phrases such as "please" and "would you mind...?"

CHAPTER 6

Timeliness

In the professional arena, a specific time is given for when either you or your work is expected to appear. First there is the *directive*, then there is the *appearance*. First the appointment is made, then you appear for the appointment. First you are given an assignment and due date, then your assignment appears on the due date. Timeliness applies only to these appearances. What happens between the directive and the appearance is irrelevant, and that is why your professors are not interested in excuses when something or someone does not appear when it should.

Expecting timeliness for appointments and classes is not being a stickler, nor does it necessarily reflect rigidity. Punctuality communicates that you value the time that the other person is giving you and how that time will benefit your development. It also shows your respect for colleagues and the learning environment. When you are a professional in the workforce, being on time and prepared communicates that you value your clients, are invested in their care and well-being, and are willing to put forth your best effort to help them. It is worth mentioning that timeliness is also culturally variable; different cultures have different relationships with time. As such, you may experience timeliness in very different ways with different faculty.

It may be helpful for you to understand this variability when thinking about yourself as a working professional. If you have a casual attitude toward timeliness, how might that be experienced by a client who does not? I personally value and appreciate cultural differences, and it may be useful for you to pay attention to which contexts a student's lateness is problematic in and which it is not; one factor may be whether it is a group or individual context. For example, most professors rarely tolerate, let alone appreciate, tardiness in the classroom but may make cultural allowances and be more flexible for individual appointments.

Apart from showing up to class on time, submitting your assignments on time is also extremely important. Doing so shows that you prioritize your learning and can effectively budget your time to meet deadlines. It reflects responsibility, reliability, and maturity. You will inevitably encounter unfortunate obstacles to meeting your academic responsibilities, such as illnesses and family emergencies. The most professional approach is to anticipate that such events do arise and complete your assignments well before they are due. If you have three weeks to complete an assignment, being ill the night before is not an acceptable excuse for not having it done. Persistent lateness with assignments is a serious problem. At best, the faculty will criticize your time-management skills. At worst, it may be assumed that you simply do not care about your education or have contempt for your professor. Either way, you risk acquiring the reputation of a student who is irresponsible and unreliable.

Timeliness is also very relevant to situations that involve your completion of administrative or clerical tasks. In most work situations, the work of your coworkers will depend in part upon your work. When your work is incomplete, it affects their ability to do theirs. This is also true for the faculty in your program; they are required to track your progress throughout the program, and this will include how well you fulfill your responsibilities to submit paperwork or respond to information requests. A surefire way to destroy your reputation is to become the student who needs to be constantly reminded to do things, whether it is registering for classes, completing questionnaires, submitting required paperwork, or meeting specific deadlines. When you have to be reminded of these things, you become someone who needs to be managed, and this is endlessly frustrating to faculty and staff. They have their own work to do, and now they also have to worry about yours.

CHAPTER 7

Don't Do These Things

The following behaviors are amazingly ubiquitous, even though they are easy to avoid. They invariably irritate faculty. Know these now and save yourself some professional demerits.

- *Schedule an appointment and then not show up.* Equally problematic is canceling an appointment within minutes of when it was scheduled to start. While faculty understand that emergencies happen, showing disregard for your professor's time by being careless with appointments is a sure way to tarnish your professional reputation.

- *Expect a faculty member to schedule or reschedule an appointment on short notice.* Faculty do not think well of students who feel entitled to their time.

- *Miss a class or meeting without notifying the instructor.* Always let them know. If you have an emergency that prevents you from letting them know before class, let them know as soon as possible afterward. Please see Chapter 3, "How to Miss a Class or Meeting."

- *Talk negatively about another professor, supervisor, peer, or colleague.* This even applies to conversations among your peers. Speaking negatively of others comes off as judgmental and prompts the other person to wonder what you might say about them when they are not around. It also leaves the impression that you would rather avoid addressing issues with people, are closed off to other viewpoints or personalities, and are difficult to get along with.

- *Speak on behalf of others.* Do not come to faculty with a problem and present it as one that others in your class are also having. For example, do not go to the program chair and say that your cohort is having a hard time with a particular adjunct instructor. Even if this is true, other students are entitled to handle it in their own way or advocate for themselves. It is also frequently not true that the problem includes or affects others, and the faculty will see this claim as the student simply attempting to buttress their complaint.

- *Complain about the length, number, or difficulty of assignments and readings.* Everyone is being held to the same standard, and you do not want to give the impression that the standard is too high for you to reach. If you are having difficulty with the course requirements, please see Chapter 12, "Asking for Help."

- *Ask the instructor to soften expectations, requirements, or due dates.* Same as the previous issue.

- *Expect a faculty member to expedite something for you because you did not adequately plan ahead.* A lack of planning on your part does not constitute an emergency on your professor's part. If you are in a bind and you need something, it is okay to ask. However, acknowledge the situation that you are putting your professor in and understand that your request might not be granted.

- *Ask to change dissertation chairs for reasons other than expertise.* The way dissertation advisors are assigned varies widely by program. It may be the case that you get matched up with someone who is difficult to work with. Perhaps you find their communication style abrasive, their standards unnecessarily high, or their support unhelpful. It is unprofessional to shop around for an easier experience. See Chapter 13, "Dealing with Difficult Faculty" for advice on managing these situations.

- *Use your phone or computer during class for non-classroom activities.* Checking social media, watching videos, texting, or emailing during a class lecture is extremely disrespectful. Many students do not realize that faculty know when this is happening, but it is obvious to us. Just because the instructor has not called you out does not mean that you are getting away with it. Some faculty will choose not to confront you but still allow the experience to influence their opinion of you.

- *Use profanity.* Aside from the fact that profanity is not congruent with commonly accepted professional demeanor, you never know who might be offended.

- *Use social media carelessly or indiscriminately.* Social media is a reality of our social fabric nowadays. The large majority of graduate students use it, and many of them do not fully understand what is public and what is private. Even if you share your profile only among peers, know that they are a source of information to the faculty, and the faculty will investigate concerns. Your social media presence is necessarily an extension of your persona, and schools are beginning to create their own policies on student social media use. Possible liabilities to your professional image and demeanor include unintentional disclosure, dual relationships, threats to professional credibility, and compromising images and evidence. You do not want images of you that are frozen in time surfacing years later when you are a different person living a different life.

Be judicious with how you use social media. While you are permitted to (and should) have a private life outside of your graduate studies, know that the events of that life can affect your professional image.

CHAPTER 8

How to Ask for a
Letter of Recommendation

There are going to be plenty of times in your career when you are going to need a letter of recommendation. Some students feel shy or hesitant about asking faculty or supervisors to write letters for them because they seem very busy or overwhelmed with other tasks. Please remember that writing letters of recommendation is an instructor or supervisor's duty, so please do not hesitate to ask.

That being said, there are ways for you to reduce the burden on faculty and supervisors in writing letters for you. Minimizing the burden is related to a very important psychological phenomenon of which you will want to be very aware: Written letters are often mood-dependent. Basically, this means that you want the person writing your letter to be in the best mood possible when they are writing it so that they will be more apt to use positive adjectives and recall more quickly the good aspects of your character. The last thing you want is to annoy your referee with last-minute requests or disorganization and put them in a bad mood.

- *Identify good referees.* Identify individuals who will have a good sense of both your professionalism and competence. These should be people with whom you have worked closely and who will be able to speak to your specific strengths and areas of growth. For example, I do not recommend that you request a letter of recommendation from a professor with whom you have had only one class, unless you have had a sustained professional relationship with them beyond that class. You also do not want to ask for references from sources who are outside of your profession, such as a pastor or a professor in a different discipline. (I have received letters of recommendation from managers at Starbucks and Old Navy!) If you are applying for an internship, you definitely want to have a letter of recommendation from someone who can go beyond your academic performance and talk about your *applied skills* and your fitness for the work you will be expected to do.

- *Give them plenty of time.* This should go without saying. While each individual may require different lengths of time to complete your request, you should anticipate at least three weeks for turnaround as a starting point. A student once called me at 1 PM and said that he needed a letter of recommendation by the end of the day. While I was willing to help him out on such short notice, the letter was not as glowing as it may have been, and I resented the fact that he was so inconsiderate of my time. I also did not mention "organization" as one of his strengths.

- *Provide them with the information that they need.* It is often helpful to referees to have a current copy of your vita, as well as a description of the types of places you are applying to (for example, the type of setting and clientele and the kind of work you would be doing, etc.). You may also consider submitting additional information, such as an autobiographical statement, cover letter, career goals, personal strengths or growth areas, and a description of the position. This allows the referee to tailor the letter by mentioning specifics from your vita that may be relevant. Ask your referee what would be helpful to them.

- *Organize and communicate what you need by when you need it.* Let your referee know about the deadlines and print out copies of any forms that may need to accompany the letter. Also include the contact information for each letter recipient. Do your research and know exactly how the letters are to be prepared and submitted.

- *Educate them about the process.* Technology is changing the way we write and submit letters of recommendation. It is more and more common for them to be either emailed directly to employers or submitted using online forms. Some employers may still require hard copies with an application packet. Let your referee know what to expect. For example, if they are going to get an email notification with a link to upload the letter, confirm that you are using the email address that they prefer and alert them to look for the email (since it may get screened by a spam filter). If they have to use an online form, see if you can get a blank copy of the form to send to the referee so they will know ahead of time what they have to complete.

- *Complete as much of the clerical work as possible.* If you need to collect a number of letters to submit hard copies to several different places, prepare the envelopes ahead of time, label them, and give them to your referee. Do not just send them a list of the places and expect them to create everything. If the referee is comfortable sharing the letter with you, ask for a digital copy that you can print it on letterhead so the referee can just sign it and seal the envelope.

- *Gentle reminder.* It is okay to send a reminder to your referee if they have not completed your letter within one week of the deadline and you have already given them sufficient notice. Here is the wording that I would suggest:

Hi Dr. Williams,

I hope you are doing well.

I just wanted to follow up on the letter of recommendation that we discussed a few weeks ago for the Acme Company. The deadline is coming up on August 6th and I noticed on my profile that the letter hasn't yet been uploaded. I just wanted to be sure that you got everything you needed from me or that there wasn't a technical error. Please let me know if I can help in any way.

Thank you again for supporting me,

—Student

CHAPTER 9

Showing Your Professionalism in Interviews

In graduate school, you will have many opportunities to interview. Perhaps you will need to interview for a specialized training track, an external placement, or a research program. If you are an undergraduate student reading this ahead of interviewing for a graduate program, props to you because you will learn some important secrets. Research has proven that your first impression is the most important because every impression after that is really just a revision of the first impression. In all of these situations, your level of professionalism will be on full display. Following are some small details with big impacts during interviews:

- *Always be accommodating and available.* You do not want their first impression of you to be one of inconvenience. Do not constantly reschedule, offer limited times of availability, or be difficult to get ahold of. Always reply promptly and positively whether by phone or email.

- *Dress the part.* Never assume that the meeting will be casual unless specifically told. Use industry standards and ask a mentor if you are unsure. Attend to your hygiene, press your clothes, and bring a notebook and writing implement.

- *Arrive early but not too early.* Plan to arrive about 15 minutes early for your appointment. Always bring paper directions and a contact person's phone number in case you get lost; do not rely exclusively on your cell phone for GPS or retrieving a previous email message because you may be in an area with poor reception. If it is a brand new area, consider driving there the day before so that you become familiar with the streets and parking.

- *Do your homework.* If you did not learn everything you possibly could about the setting before applying, you should definitely do so before the interview. Read the website, paying particular attention to content that may be relevant to your work. You should also find the section about the institution or organization's history (usually found in the section called "About"), any strategic plans, initiatives, recent grants, or honors and announcements. During the interview, when something that you have come across in their materials is mentioned, you will not only have a reference point for what they are discussing but also the opportunity to align with something or ask further questions. This demonstrates that you have invested in learning about them, their identity, and what they value.

- *You are always being interviewed.* This alone might be my biggest piece of advice for interviewees. At all contact points of the process, know that you are being interviewed. When you call to schedule the appointment, you are being interviewed. When you greet the administrative assistant in the waiting room, you are being interviewed. When you are introduced to someone in passing, you are being interviewed. For my current faculty position, I was on my own between interview meetings and wandering the campus during a short break. Because it is a friendly place, someone apparently recognized I was new (and maybe out of place) and struck up a conversation with me. We talked pleasantly for about ten minutes. Later, when the offer was being made for the position, the interviewer told me that the campus minister thought I was the nicest person and was hoping that I would get the job. It was not a formal part of my interview, but my interaction with the minister on that day appeared to have influence. Always remember that you are being interviewed at all times.

- *Be prepared.* Have copies of any materials they may be interested in, such as your curriculum vita or resume, a portfolio, or other work products.

- *Always project positivity and enthusiasm at all points of the process.* Never point out flaws, play hard-to-get, be confrontational or arrogant, or let on that you were more impressed with another agency or program. These behaviors do not make them want you more.

Even if you know during the interview that you do not want the position, the people you interact with will necessarily become part of your professional network, and you may have further contact with them in other professional settings (and maybe even in other job interviews).

- *Never leave an interview without asking questions.* Asking questions shows that you have invested in the interview process and want to learn as much about them as possible. It also shows that you are thoughtful and deliberate. If you leave an interview without asking questions, it will seem like you do not care.

  ➢ *Three questions minimum, five questions maximum.* You want to appear interested, not obsessive.

  ➢ *Write your questions down ahead of time.* This helps prevent your mind from going blank when being put on the spot. Write down a few extra questions in case some of your questions get answered during the interview. Feel free to take notes when getting responses and thank them for answering your questions.

  ➢ *Do not ask questions when the answers are readily available.* Asking a question about information that is front and center on their website shows them that you really did not prepare. If you have done your homework, you can develop questions from that research. This shows that you have spent time learning about them and what they do and want more details or a personalized answer.

➤ *Do not ask canned questions.* There are many websites offering advice on "good" interview questions. When I hear them, I roll my eyes on the inside. Take the time to personalize the questions. The following are some examples:

Not So Good	Better
What are the strengths and weaknesses of your program?	I see that this program is relatively young. What have been the biggest challenges in getting started and what really helped you?
Where do you see the program in five years?	I like that the clinical services here are highly specialized in working with children. If there was a specific service or population you would be interested in adding to the program in the future, what would it be?
What do you like most about working here?	I can see that working at a place with such an emphasis on customer care is appealing. Are there other reasons why you like working here?
What makes a student successful in this program?	I know that this program has a strong emphasis on research. What qualities or skills should I work on to be successful with the research requirements?

CHAPTER 10

Withdrawing Applications and Resigning

I n your program, you may have opportunities to apply externally for work experience as part of your program requirements, such as a practicum, internship, or externship. Many students feel uncomfortable turning down offers or withdrawing applications. Perhaps they feel like they are letting others down, think that they are spoiling chances for future opportunities, or believe that they owe the agency something because they were offered a position. These feelings are understandable in students who are often very eager to please. However, accepting offers to avoid feeling guilt may thwart you from moving toward what you really want.

Most employers know and understand that they are competing for applicants when making hiring decisions. They know that when they are interviewing an applicant the applicant is simultaneously interviewing them. When done professionally, a withdrawal causes no hard feelings. Turning down a position is more straightforward than you think if you can stop yourself from overthinking it. Please note that this advice does *not* apply to situations where you are matched with a placement through a contractual agreement. Here are a few points to keep in mind:

- Everything you do between submitting an application and accepting an offer you do as an "applicant" (though in some situations you may be referred to as a "candidate" at a certain stage of the process). Thus, do not think of this process as turning anyone down. Rather, remember that you are simply withdrawing your application.

- Withdrawing an application can be done over the phone or in an email. An email message is perfectly fine and more common because you can be sure to plan out what you want to say.

- Write only one message. Do not write multiple messages to multiple people. If there were multiple people involved in your interview, you can address the message to either the primary contact person or the entire group. Do not send the message individually to multiple recipients to avoid giving the impression that you are open to discussing your decision with some people and not others.

- Keep the message brief. One short or medium-sized paragraph is fine.

- Never say anything negative or critical in your withdrawal message. Always maintain a positive tone. (Note: An exception to this advice may be if you feel that you were unfairly discriminated against during the interview process and are planning to file a complaint with their equal opportunity office. In this case, you may or may not wish to tell them about your complaint.)

- Do not feel compelled to make excuses or justify your decision. Frankly, you do not owe them an explanation.

- Express your gratitude for the time they invested reviewing your application and interviewing you.

- Say something positive about the setting or the people that you met with.

- Wish them well.

Here is an example:

Dear Dr. Lao,

I hope this message finds you well and enjoying the nice break in the rainy weather that we've had in the past few days.

It is with great regret that I am writing to you today to withdraw my application for the coordinator position. It was a very difficult decision for me because I really enjoyed seeing the facility, learning about your cutting-edge program, and meeting all of the friendly staff. Anyone would be truly lucky to work there, and I really appreciate the time you took in reviewing my application and organizing the interview. If my circumstances change in the future, I would love the opportunity to consider other positions in your agency as they arise.

I hope you have great success with your coordinator search.

Sincerely,

Peggy Sue

Resigning

In graduate school, your field placements or internships are contractual, meaning that they are of fixed duration and you will not be resigning without the permission of your graduate program. However, if you are in a situation where you can resign, keep in mind that it is also a relatively easy process. The message is brief, business-like, and professional. There is no need to provide an explanation or other information about where you are going next. In some cases, employers will provide an opportunity to give feedback in an exit interview, though the extent to which you do this is at your own discretion.

Because they initiate formal action from human resources and become part of your employee file, letters of resignation often have to be signed by you and submitted in hard copy (though some employers may accept an email or email attachment). Here are some points for a letter of resignation:

- If possible, write the letter on official company letterhead with proper date and addressee format.

- Address the letter to your immediate supervisor. Add "cc" lines for human resources and any others who may be directly impacted by your resignation (for example, department heads or project managers).

- After the salutation, directly state your intention of resigning with the date that your resignation is effective. Do not open a letter of resignation with a pleasantry.

- Two weeks is typically the minimum amount of notice to give to employers for your resignation. However, in some cases it is more professional and appreciated when you give more. The professional response is to make sure that your departure disrupts the program as little as possible.

- Include a brief thank-you for the work opportunity and the growth that you experienced.

After you submit your resignation, maintain a positive and appreciative attitude. The degree to which you disclose your reasons for leaving is at your discretion, though note that it can always be phrased positively: "This move is right for my family at this time," "I am taking a new step for my career," and "I am looking forward to some new opportunities" are all appropriate messages that do not reveal specifics.

If you are leaving a position and are upset with your coworkers, disgruntled about unfair treatment, or displeased with the practices or policies of the agency, you may have the opportunity to provide feedback during an exit interview. Depending on your level of comfort or interest in providing this feedback, you can also discuss it with your supervisor. Never complain to the people who are served by the agency (such as clients, students, or patients) about your reasons for leaving by blaming the agency, slandering coworkers, or criticizing supervisors. Stirring up conflict as you walk out the door is petty, spiteful, and passive-aggressive. Moreover, it will undoubtedly backfire because your professional community is smaller than you think; such behavior will become part of your reputation.

CHAPTER 11

Getting Feedback

Developing professionalism is an ongoing process. You never get to a place where you "achieve" professionalism and can then stop working at it; there will always be opportunities to show professionalism and respond to new and interesting challenges, and these are necessarily opportunities for growth. Each new situation that you enter may expose you to a different interpersonal style and set of expectations. Your recognition of and adaptability to these challenges will be facilitated by applying the broad principles of professional etiquette, reading verbal and nonverbal communications, and anticipating needs and reactions.

While these strategies are important, you still may not know how others experience your behaviors without getting their actual opinion on how you are doing. Professors will give you feedback on your mastery of the learning objectives (your competence) because that is the charge of the courses that they teach. However, they may not comment on your professionalism unless it is particularly exceptional or concerning. If you are in a program where you do not receive narrative evaluations, then you will probably get this feedback only if the professor pulls you aside or you ask for it.

Feedback on professionalism is more likely to be found in evaluations from practice-based program activities, such as internships, field placements, or work-study that is performed in the community. In these settings, you are operating alongside professionals in your field for a limited amount of time. In addition to training you in certain skills, they are implicitly tasked with "trying you out" as a coworker and colleague, which makes them very interested in sending feedback about your professionalism to your program.

While positive feedback is always nice to receive, the negative (or "constructive") feedback is equally important because it directs your growth. It is also important to note that faculty have varying styles of delivering feedback. Some faculty are gentle with feedback, some are uncomfortable with it and may beat around the bush, and some can be brutally direct. Regardless of how they deliver the feedback, note that you have some control over how you respond.

It is important for you to remember that feedback is inherently part of a developmental process and not an ultimate statement about your character. We do not expect you to be perfect. Rather, we expect that you will use missteps to learn and grow. We know that there are things you do not understand and that you may have come from contexts that do not have the same expectations with regard to professionalism. Indeed, among the students I am most fond of are those who struggled significantly with professional issues early on, worked with me with an open attitude, and demonstrated considerable growth and maturity by the time of graduation.

Said more plainly, *how you respond to feedback is much more important than the content of the feedback itself.* Approaching these challenges with openness and a desire to improve is a hallmark of professionalism and is seen as such by the faculty.

Constructive Feedback

When you are not aware of unwritten professional expectations, getting constructive feedback about them can take you by surprise. This can feel very confusing, like being caught off guard by a strong gust of wind. Following that initial confusion, there are typically three ways that students respond: defensiveness, withdrawal, and acceptance. Interestingly, both defensiveness and withdrawal are driven in part by *confirmation bias*, which is a psychological heuristic that describes why it is easier to accept information that is congruent with our self-perception and harder to accept information that is incongruent with our self-perception.

Defensiveness

Defensiveness usually occurs when constructive feedback does not match our positive self-perception, making the feedback difficult to internalize. It would be natural to expect this response in students who are more confident or have a broader life experience. If you see yourself as a competent person trying to do the right thing, then it can be difficult to hear otherwise. Maybe you were really trying to help a peer, but the instructor was not pleased with how you challenged them in class. Perhaps you truly value being dependable and reliable, but your supervisor was not pleased with your lack of follow-through. Maybe you really did not think it would be a big deal to miss the group presentations, but the professor felt very disrespected.

It is true that good intentions are an important ingredient of a professional attitude. However, good intentions are not always enough; they do not guarantee that your behavior will be consistent with professional expectations. Some students get into trouble wanting to do the right thing without knowing what the right thing is.

It is normal to experience uncomfortable emotions, such as embarrassment, guilt, sadness, anxiety, disappointment, or shame when getting constructive feedback. Defensiveness acts as a kind of safeguard against these experiences and can show up as arguing, making excuses, or trying to find loopholes in policy. If we can instead make the situation someone else's fault or otherwise prove that the observed behavior was *not* indeed unprofessional, then we do not have to feel these uncomfortable emotions.

It is easier to feel angry and either argue or deflect blame than it is to accept that we made a mistake and feel shame or embarrassment. However, the position you will necessarily find yourself in when being defensive is trying to convince your professors that you know better than they do. It may be true that your intention was misread, but this is irrelevant at this point in the process. Arguing and deflecting blame are not compatible with responsibility and accountability; they will only worsen your predicament. Said another way, defensiveness is an emotional process unrelated to the situation.

Withdrawal

The other end of the spectrum of responding to constructive feedback—opposite to the impulse to fight back—is slinking away by avoiding or withdrawing. This response is more typical in students who lack confidence or struggle with self-worth and thus take the feedback very personally; instead of its being an invitation to a behavioral adjustment, it feels like a judgment of their entire self. If you are your own worst critic—even if you have had ample experiences of positive feedback—then constructive feedback becomes fodder for your self-punishment. When embarrassment, guilt, and shame feel intolerable, students sometimes use avoidance or withdrawal so they do not have to feel vulnerable in front of their faculty or peers. They may feel on some level that if they can punish themselves enough then they will change.

However, withdrawal is problematic because—like defensiveness—it suspends the process of learning from your mistakes and reinforces the polarized notion that you are either perfect or a failure. It also necessarily undermines the role of relationships in personal growth. As discussed throughout this book, professionalism is a relational construct: It exists primarily within the interactions that we have with others. Learning to grow in this context can and should involve and be facilitated by the very relationships that experience these mistakes. When you avoid the problem, you are also avoiding the solution.

ACCEPTANCE

What makes acceptance different from both defensiveness and withdrawal is that acceptance does not operate on emotional avoidance. Acceptance means that the student accepts any unwanted discomfort that may come from difficult or constructive feedback, foregoing the temptation to argue or withdraw and instead focusing on moving forward. In other words, if the discomfort does not need to be pushed away then we can be more flexible in our responding. Apologizing, owning the misstep, and pledging to do better are integral to this process. This truly reflects responsibility and accountability and recognizes the role of your superiors in your professional training. It makes you teachable.

Acceptance also opens the window for you to clarify any misperceived intent. Following the acceptance of the feedback, faculty typically welcome knowing more about your process and can use it to further your professional development. Consider this statement from a student accepting some constructive feedback:

> *I am very sorry for missing the group meeting yesterday. It was not my intention to be disrespectful or irresponsible, but I understand now how it came across that way. I was feeling very worried about falling behind in my paperwork and thought you might appreciate my taking the time to get caught up so that my report could be submitted on time. I realize that I should have considered a different strategy.*

In this example, the student's clarification of the intent to please the supervisor opens an opportunity to discuss some larger professional issues. For example, if a student approached me with this statement, I would want to help them by discussing (a) the factors that are affecting the student's ability to complete tasks on time, (b) the importance and relevance of the group meeting, and (c) what I might be inadvertently doing to make the student fearful of talking about falling behind. For this last point, it is important for me as a supervisor to know where my students are struggling so that I can adequately help them. If the student hesitates in coming forward with a problem, then it can cause problems down the road. Harboring fear in a supervisory relationship and hiding challenges can prevent professional growth.

The student's acceptance of the situation makes me want to talk about how I can change to help them through this issue. It draws me in. After all, it is very likely that if the student does not address their fear of disappointing me, they will carry that same fear to their next professional setting. This obviously means placing some trust in the supervisor because it requires willingness to be a little vulnerable. In sum, the movement forward here necessarily involves self-honesty in the form of accepting both the discomfort from the feedback and the responsibility for doing better.

CHAPTER 12

Asking for Help

G raduate school will likely be very different from your undergraduate experience. Both the increased rigor and the expectations around professionalism will challenge your typical study strategies and general approach to relating with others. You may have long-standing habits such as procrastination and all-night cramming that paid off in the end, or perhaps you were able to find study guides, primers, and summaries of important texts. Maybe you were able to miss classes because your instructor either did not notice or did not care and you could rely on the text content to pass the tests.

Even if you had great study habits and excellent time management, the greater breadth and depth of information that you have to learn in graduate school will require some adjustment. We usually assume that this adjustment process begins in the first year in our program; students spend that time getting used to the homework demands, the intense schedule, and a new way of relating to peers and faculty. As they progress through the program, the homework demands continue to increase, the schedule gets more complicated, and the expectations around interpersonal interactions become more refined.

It is also true that expectations for self-sufficiency are higher in graduate school. That is why some of the advice in this book encourages you to find answers on your own prior to going to faculty. However, this expectation can also create a serious problem for struggling students *who believe that they have to do everything on their own.*

Most students get into hot water when they continue trying to solve their own problems when doing so is not working. They may try various time-management strategies to meet the deadlines at their field placement only to still miss them. They may try to manage growing discomfort or resentment with their supervisor only to find it boiling over and coming out in their behaviors. They may try different studying strategies for a difficult class only to find themselves getting further and further behind.

You should not suffer in silence when an issue is negatively affecting your education. If you find yourself feeling alone in the midst of your struggles, that is a sign that you need to reach out and ask for help. It is true that your faculty are going to make you struggle in order to learn, but they are not trying to defeat you. Professors in graduate programs hold a high bar and want to help you reach it. Indeed, most professors would prefer to help you than fail you.

Reflecting on personal barriers that may get in the way of asking for help is an important exercise. It facilitates the awareness needed to effectively direct your behavior in more productive ways. This kind of self-exploration is not always easy, but it will identify the situations—and the associated thoughts and feelings—that need to be confronted. The exercise on pages 68 and 69 can help you with this.

Imposter Syndrome

Many of the psychological barriers listed in the Self-Inventory exercise are characteristics of *imposter syndrome*. This phenomenon describes the thoughts and feelings someone gets when they believe they are out of place or do not belong. For example, a college student may believe that there was a mistake during the admissions process and that they are not supposed to be at the university. They may constantly fear that at any moment someone is going to discover they are an "imposter" and expose them as a fake. It is not uncommon for these students to see themselves as less intelligent or less competent than their peers and to experience a deep insecurity about not being good enough.

Sometimes students struggling with imposter syndrome will try to compensate for these insecurities by striving for perfection, even when it becomes counterproductive. Others may instead choose to withdraw, avoid, and hide when they fear that someone will find their mistakes.

Imposter syndrome tends to be common in women, racial and ethnic minorities, and first-generation college students because it is what we call a contextual factor. That is, the messages that inform our beliefs about various groups of people can be found in the social context. Our society is replete with messages, images, and stories that portray women and racial and ethnic minorities as inferior. There is no reason for a female or minority student to believe that those messages and beliefs will be any different when they enter a graduate program. For first-generation college students, the dynamic is slightly different: They are venturing beyond the level of education and training of their own family. Sometimes first-generation college students experience

Exercise

Self-Inventory of Barriers to Seeking Help

It may be helpful for you to do a preventive self-inventory of any possible barriers to seeking help. Doing so can help you anticipate and recognize situations where you may need to challenge these barriers to be successful.

1. Please review the following beliefs about seeking help and indicate which ones you have experienced either now or in the past.

    ❑   If I ask for help I will appear weak.
    ❑   I don't want to disappoint the faculty.
    ❑   The faculty do not care or won't believe me.
    ❑   The faculty cannot help me with this issue.
    ❑   I am a failure if I cannot do it myself.
    ❑   I should be able to do this on my own.
    ❑   I'm worried that I will be negatively judged.
    ❑   I do not deserve the help.
    ❑   _____

2. List the individuals involved in situations where you felt hesitant or resistant to asking for help, even if you eventually did so.

    •   _____
    •   _____
    •   _____
    •   _____

3. Briefly describe these situations. What were you struggling with? How was the struggle getting in the way of what you were wanting to do?

_____

_____

_____

_____

_____

_____

4. Reflect on the list in #2 and see if any patterns emerge. What are the characteristics of the people that you listed? Were they instructors or supervisors whom you experienced as judgmental or unapproachable? Do any of them remind you of people you know personally, such as an overbearing grandfather, an emotionally distant aunt, or a friend who betrayed you? Are they mostly men? Women? Did their racial or ethnic backgrounds make it uncomfortable in any way for you to approach them for help?

5. Reflect on your responses to #3 and see if any patterns emerge. Are certain situations more likely to elicit resistance to asking for help? Do they involve struggles that you have with specific skills or areas of practice? Do the situations start out the same way or follow a predictable pattern of events? What do you think the situations have in common?

negative attitudes from members of their family who might think they are trying to "leave them behind" or are "selling out." Some first-generation college students might feel guilty for their education's financial or emotional cost on their family.

Whether you are struggling with imposter syndrome or have one or more of these psychological barriers to seeking help, it is important to find a way through these discomforts so that you can effectively enlist the assistance that will make your success more likely. Without being able to provide you with counseling through the text on these pages, my most direct advice in these situations is to let yourself feel like a failure and then go and ask for help anyway, or believe that the faculty will not help you and still ask for their assistance. The beliefs and feelings are not the problem. Avoiding help is the problem. I expect that practicing this over time will make it easier for you. Even if it does not get easier, at least you will be getting the help that you need. If this strategy does not work for you, personal therapy or counseling likely will.

Talking About Your Learning Needs

Most faculty understand that learning styles are just as variable as communication styles. Some students learn best through reading, some through examples, and some through discussion and analysis. As such, faculty are often amenable to students asking for help or providing direction on how they can get the most out of a class, supervision, or research program. Here are some points to remember when asking for help:

1. Your goal is specifically to maximize your own learning. The message that you want to send about meeting with faculty is that you care about the content and value the learning experience. You want to be able to get as much out of it as possible.

2. With #1 in mind, keep your discussion focused on what you need to do differently and not what the instructor or supervisor needs to do differently. This does two things. First, it exemplifies responsibility and accountability by showing the professor that you are taking charge of your own learning. Second, this approach minimizes the chances that your professor or supervisor may become defensive, at which point the discussion could become counterproductive. See the table on the next page for some examples.

3. Ask for other sources of learning that can supplement the course material. In addition to seeking advice and assistance from the professor, show that you are also willing to do more if necessary.

University Resources

Most universities provide a host of student support services designed to maximize academic success. Writing centers, math centers, tutoring, mentoring, research assistance, peer support, and psychological counseling may be available to you at no cost. These offices may provide drop-in hours, workshops, support groups, or individualized assistance and are staffed by individuals who have a sincere interest in being helpful. Sometimes students just need some tips on time

The Issue	Not So Good	Better
Faculty is not responsive.	"You don't answer my emails quick enough."	"I need a little more guidance as I work on this project."
The lectures are not useful.	"Your lectures could use more examples."	"Sometimes examples are helpful for me in learning to apply the theory."
You don't like the book.	"The book is not very good."	"I am having a hard time relating to the author's way of presenting the material."
Your grade on a paper was lower than expected.	"I think I deserve a better grade."	"What can I do differently on the next assignment to do better?"
The feedback is confusing.	"Your feedback is not useful."	"Could we speak sometime about your feedback, so I can understand it better?"
You're falling behind.	"There's too much work in this class."	"I seem to be having difficulty keeping up in the class."

management, organizational skills, and learning strategies. Others may benefit from more individualized help, ongoing support, or guidance. In any case, it makes sense to take advantage of the help that is readily available.

Another important resource for students who may be struggling is the office of disability support services. Unfortunately, many students are still influenced by the lingering stigma of disability status, and this is sometimes a barrier to their seeking help through this office. For some of the students who persistently struggle in our program, I sometimes wonder if that struggle is caused by an undiagnosed learning disability. The disability office has as its mission to help students with disabilities gain equal access to the educational opportunities. When a student has a documented disability, the office becomes your advocate for your rights under the Americans with Disabilities Act and outlines accommodations that are available that can maximize your success. Examples are having extra time for assignments, receiving classroom materials or lectures in alternative formats, and taking tests in distraction-free environments. While accommodations do not ease educational expectations or grading criteria, they increase the opportunities to demonstrate achievement for students whose success might otherwise have been limited by a disability.

Reading Your Professor's Door

If you need something from your professor, first try to visit during their scheduled office hours. If you cannot and you approach your professor's office, know that you can read their "door language." If the door is wide open, it usually means that you are free to stop by with anything, even if it is just to say hello or share some unimportant news. If the door is only slightly open, it means that you can interrupt if you need something, but please do not stop by just to chat or small talk. Sometimes I leave my door open only a crack, and this signals that I am here for anything urgent but otherwise please do not disturb me. If my door is closed but you know that I am here, you had better not interrupt me unless there is an emergency. I will not even answer the door if you knock unless you are also yelling about the building being on fire.

If you need something from your professor but decide it is not important enough to interrupt them, then you will need to select a different medium. If it is a form or something else you need signed, you can either slip it under the door or use their faculty mailbox. If it is a question, it might be better to email. If you need to consult on an issue or otherwise get some advice, it is best to schedule something in advance if possible. In fact, a lot of my students will even "schedule" having their forms signed by asking me when it would be okay to stop by the office. Planning these kinds of tasks ahead of time will help the faculty member budget their time and will save the both of you a lot of hassle.

When scheduling a time to consult with a professor on an issue, it can be useful to give a brief description of the matter, ask the professor if this is something in their wheelhouse, and give an estimate of how much time you think it may take. In addition, some faculty will appreciate knowing what kind of assistance would be most useful for you. For example, are you looking for specific advice? Do you want them to help you develop some options or problem solve? Do you just need support?

CHAPTER 13

Dealing with Difficult Faculty

I guarantee that during your graduate career you will have to deal with someone in a position of authority whom you do not like, whether it is a supervisor, professor, or advisor. In fact, because you are human, this reality will follow you around for the rest of your life. Everyone has unique characteristics, values, expectations, and styles of communication. When we experience someone as difficult, it is usually because there is a mismatch between the individual and ourselves in one or more of these areas. When this occurs with faculty, you may experience them as rude, offensive, overly strict, or critical, and it may even feel as though these negative qualities are being personally directed at you.

You may also have professors who are not skilled in teaching because not all schools and programs prioritize teaching skills in their faculty. For example, many research-oriented schools want faculty who can obtain grants and publish articles and place less emphasis on their teaching and advising skills. The faculty may have varying levels of interest in your personal success and will put varying levels of effort into their lectures and assignments. In these situations, you may feel that the professor is incompetent and the class is a waste of your time, or you may find yourself being argumentative in class.

You may even have professors who seem hostile to students from certain social groups. This includes professors who discuss views that are racist, sexist, homophobic, transphobic, ableist, classist, nationalist, and so on. Similarly, when students in the class make negative comments about vulnerable groups or populations, the professor may do little or nothing to defend them.

Professors may also be disparaging toward certain political or religious groups while claiming protection under the First Amendment right of freedom of speech or academic freedom. These are important pillars of democracy and allow professors to say and study what is consistent with their pedagogical and intellectual commitments without fear of recourse. However, professors have an equal responsibility to (1) treat all students with dignity and respect, (2) create a classroom environment that is conducive to learning, and (3) protect the freedom and right of students to disagree. Importantly, academic freedom does *not* permit professors to threaten or harass students, treat them differently based on their identity or affiliation, or penalize them for disagreeing. If you are experiencing any of these behaviors, please consider the advice in the next chapter.

Challenges to an Open Learning Stance

When you have trouble getting along with faculty members, you are at risk of acting out in unprofessional ways. If you dread going to class, you may start arriving late or skipping altogether. You may become apathetic about the course content, daydream during class, or put less effort into your assignments and exams. You might also feel contempt for the professor, prompting you to behave arrogantly, talk negatively about the professor to others, or dismiss the value of their knowledge. Avoidance, dishonesty, and cynicism are also risks. In other words, there is a risk of acting out when struggling with these kinds of difficulties because the behaviors communicate what we are feeling. When faculty observe these problematic behaviors in the academic context, they have no reason to believe that you might not also display them in your future employment context.

When you do not like your teachers, it is very easy to slip into a mindset that is more centered on your frustration than on learning, and here is where it becomes a problem: *If you are unable to identify something that you can learn from someone you do not like, it means that you have not yet suspended your belief that you are better than them.* Your humility and openness are then gone. Regardless of whether or not it is true that you are better than them, believing that you are necessarily blunts your learning capacity.

Your task as a student is to maintain focus on your learning objectives irrespective of how you may feel toward your professor or the course content. Your right to disagree with alternative views does not absolve you of your responsibility to learn them. Learning how to walk this fine line is an exercise in several important professional values, such as working with differences, adaptation, lifelong learning, and open mindedness. Indeed, a hallmark of professionalism is the attitude of lifelong learning, which means understanding that you will never understand everything and that every moment provides an opportunity to grow. It is a misfortune when this understanding is lost, especially when it happens in an educational context.

Moving Beyond Liking to Learning

In my Professional Seminar class, I ask students to rank the learning activities of the program in order of their usefulness to their own professional development. Examples of learning activities include the dissertation, comprehensive exams, practicum placements, coursework, mentoring, and so on. Generally, they put at the bottom of their list activities they thought were pointless, but in actuality, these were aspects of the program where they struggled. I then ask the students to break up into small groups, pick one of their bottom choices, and make a case for how that activity actually *helped* them professionally—advising them not to let their discussions devolve into unprofessional complaining and blaming.

Interestingly, once students find a way to get out of the tendency to complain about the activities they thought were pointless, they are able to identify concrete growth that occurred from something they found challenging. Their "like" for something became separated from its usefulness. I do this exercise as preparation for internship interviews so that students know what to say when questioned about these activities by their interviewers.

Learning from program activities that you do not like is no different than learning from faculty whom you do not like. Being the judge and jury of your faculty communicates that only you decide when you are teachable. This is a dangerous place for a student to be. Having an open learning stance does not require that we agree with what faculty purport, or accept their teaching as true. This is not about right and wrong. Rather, what larger lessons might exist in the struggles that we have with values that conflict with our own? What exercise in professionalism is waiting for us when we open ourselves to what we do not like? What might someone else see in us that we cannot? If you see yourself as above your education, then it precludes you from such exploration.

Moving Forward

The exercise on pages 80 and 81 is constructed to reveal any personal barriers that may be preventing you from moving forward in a difficult training experience. The awareness will hopefully change your perspective and make it easier to endure your interactions with them. Depending on what shows up for you, there are usually two options for what you may want to do next: Accept the difficulty or address the issue.

ACCEPT THE DIFFICULTY

This option may be preferred if (a) the issue is not seriously interfering with your education, (b) you can effectively manage your professional demeanor by using the insight from the exercise, and (c) you do not care about having to further interact with the person after the conclusion of your time together. Accepting the situation does not mean that you are giving in, agreeing with, or enabling the person. The professor is not right by default. Moreover, it actually does not matter who is right and who is wrong. The format of your education is necessarily based on a master-student model, with the master determining the learning objectives, the learning methods, and the evaluation of the student. Sure, the good professors also consider themselves students

Exercise
Challenging Assumptions

Our interpersonal difficulty with someone often reveals more about ourselves than it does the other person. I would challenge you with the following thought exercise, adapted for opening your attitude toward a professor with whom you are having a hard time:

1. Think of a professor or supervisor with whom you are struggling. What thoughts do you notice showing up when you think about them? Maybe it is something like, *They don't know what they're talking about*, *I can't stand the way he talks down to students*, or *She needs to listen more to what the students say*. Take a moment to notice what your mind says about the person.

2. For the sake of this exercise, take the answer to #1 and make it the opposite. If you thought the professor does not know what they are talking about, construct the thought, *They really know what they're talking about*. Explore that thought and consider what it would mean *if it were true*. Do not try to convince yourself that it *is* true; just think about what it would mean if it were. Would it mean that you were wrong? Would it mean that you were less compassionate than you thought you were? You will need to step out of your own frame of refer-

ence to fully explore this step; it can be difficult because you will notice that your mind tries to convince you not to consider it. *No! He really doesn't know anything!* your mind will say. This is just defensiveness, so try to move beyond it. What that thought is trying to defend against might be found in Step 3.

3. Notice what shows up emotionally after constructing the opposite thought in Step 2. It would be normal to experience something like anger, disgust, guilt, embarrassment, powerlessness, fear, and so on. The emotional reaction is often the barrier that prevents us from seeing our way forward in these situations. Notice what this is because it will probably show up again in the future with the next person you do not like.

4. Now set the thoughts aside and come up with something concrete that you have learned or can learn from this professor. If your answer is "I learned how not to teach a class" or "I learned what a terrible supervisor is," then you have more work to do. Dig deep to identify the ways that this person could help you grow. How might their views help you understand the context of your own views? Does their lack of knowledge force you to develop your own learning? What kind of exercise are you getting in managing your behavior in this relationship? What virtue are you developing?

because they are lifelong learners. However, because of the power differential, the professor will always have the final determination simply because their job is to deliver the educational experience. It does not make sense to struggle against this reality.

ADDRESS THE ISSUE

If the difficulty you are having with a professor is negatively affecting your education, making it difficult to control your behaviors, or involves a long-term relationship (for example, with a clinical supervisor or thesis chair), then it would behoove you to establish a bridge with the person. Before going into these strategies, it is important to raise your awareness around how your own tendency to blame others may play a role in this process.

It is very natural to badly want the other person to do something differently; however, there are two problems with this approach. The first is that an interpersonal conflict between two people is almost always a two-person tango: Each person is bringing something to the interaction. The second problem is that blaming the other person will only increase the chances of their becoming defensive.

The optimal and most professional scenario for two people working out an issue occurs when both parties fully acknowledge their own part and pledge to adjust. When you take ownership—even if you have to stretch what feels true—you are offering your vulnerability as a gift to the relationship. This sets up the best possible chance for the other person to do the same, and from there you can enter a discussion about what each of you needs from the other. Keep in mind, though, that because of the power differential, there may be varying levels of willingness among faculty to do their own acknowledging of how they contribute to the problem, in which case you may be doing a lot of the changing on your own. Even if the faculty member does not own their part or express any interest in changing, your response is still the more professional one.

Here are a few points that may help guide your messaging when trying to broach the issue with a faculty member:

- *Keep the focus on the desire to improve.* Frame the conversation in a way that communicates your desire to be a better student.

- *Confront the problem, not the person.* Discuss the interactional sequences that feel problematic without trying to analyze what the other person is doing. Do this by describing behaviors (what was done or said) without using any character labels (for example, "rude" or "impatient").

- *Discuss what you have already tried to make things better.* Mentioning what you have tried already shows that you are invested in the relationship and want it to improve.

- *Be willing to hear some feedback that may feel uncomfortable.* If a faculty member has a concern about you and you open this door, they are probably going to use the opportunity to let you know.

- *Stand up for yourself.* If the faculty member is resistant to adjusting in some ways that are important to you, share your experience in the relationship. Doing so is a form of self-validation and self-advocacy. The process begins with identifying your emotional reactions in the context of their specific behaviors and communicating them as such. For example, "I feel disempowered when you reject my input for this project." The beauty of leading with a feeling word is that it cannot be disputed; no one can tell you that you do not feel disempowered. (If instead you led with telling them that they are overly rejecting, they can certainly argue with you about that!)

Note that the purpose of this sharing is not to compel them to change, because their behaviors are never going to be under your control. Rather, a statement like this establishes the impact that the person is having on you, leaving the ball in their court. They can now decide if that is how they want to be coming off. Regardless of which way they go, having shared your experience necessarily claims space in the relationship.

- *Appeal to a third party.* If you find yourself at an impasse with a faculty member and have been unsuccessful in your attempts to address the issue, you may consider enlisting a third party to help facilitate a discussion. If the issue negatively affects your education and the faculty member is responsible for that education, then it is appropriate to go to the faculty member's immediate superior, such as a supervisor or department chair. In some cases, the chair will attempt to form a solution on their own, but they may instead offer to help mediate the problem by facilitating a discussion. Should you take this route, discuss this with the faculty member first and attempt to enlist their support. Know that the chair will not be there to advocate for you or take your side in the dispute; rather, they can be helpful in both clarifying the expectations being placed on you and helping the faculty member see your concerns more clearly.

Grade Challenges

Grade challenges refer to any situation where you seek a review of a grade that you received for an assignment, paper, exam, or course. The process usually begins with asking the faculty member directly about the justification for the grade or to better understand how the grade was determined. If, following this discussion, you feel as though the grade was still unfair and the professor is unwilling to either change it or provide another opportunity (such as allowing you to submit revisions or another paper), most universities have a due process mechanism for challenging grades. You can probably find the policy and procedure in your university catalog or student handbook; it may include a description of the steps involved, such as having the assignment independently reviewed by a program chair, dean, or faculty committee.

It is important to highlight that grade-challenge procedures are designed for situations where the grading appears to be unfair, such as the professor showing a personal bias, using grading criteria that were not specified in the assignment instructions or syllabus, or removing points without adequate explanation and justification. It is not appropriate to use grade challenges because you disagree with your professor on how many points you should earn. Professors have full discretion in evaluating your level of learning. To argue otherwise is to say that you know more than your professor does, and this is very unprofessional.

When I was in graduate school, I received a lower-than-expected grade on a paper. When I asked the professor about it, she explained that I did not address several points relevant to the topic. However, when I reviewed the assignment instructions, those points were not clearly specified. I felt that I was being penalized for poorly written assignment instructions. The conversation with the instructor began gently, but as I fixated on the problem with the instructions (that is, making it her fault so that I did not have to feel inadequate), I became more argumentative. I was trying to tell her what she meant when she wrote the instructions. This is the absurdity that defensiveness can lead to. It was truly an important lesson for me because I was missing the bigger picture. Who was right and who was wrong was irrelevant—the professor was providing me with a learning opportunity through the grade itself. I had clearly fell short in her eyes, and I needed to adapt my approach to doing assignments if I wanted to do better. There was no end game in wanting to triumph over the professor.

Splitting Faculty

If you are in a situation where you are trying to get something from a faculty member but they are not giving it to you, it may be tempting to go around them and ask someone else. Situations like this may include seeking an exception to the policy for dissertation committee members, registering for the course section that all of your friends are in, or getting some kind of non-required accommodation to a training activity that will make your life easier (for example, switching to a supervisor with a later appointment time so that you can sleep in). In most situations, one person will have the authority to make decisions that directly affect your experience in the program. Going around that one person when you do not get what you want is very unprofessional.

A student once accepted an external training placement but later received another offer from a different placement he preferred more. Because I oversee the placements in the program, the student asked me how to best renege on the former agreement so that he could take the latter offer. I informed him that, unfortunately, he must honor the first placement; he had formed a verbal contract with his acceptance, and the site had planned accordingly. Unsatisfied with this response, he went to another faculty member to ask for advice on how to get out of the situation. Having full respect for roles in the department, the other faculty member redirected him to me and copied me on the email. When I confronted the student about the issue, he proffered that he was only trying to get another opinion and was planning on talking with me about it further with any new information that he received from the other faculty member.

This is called splitting faculty. The student attempted to override one faculty member by using another faculty member against them, all in order to get what he wants. In the student's mind, the best possible scenario was if he could have come back to me with "Dr. Gonzales said that this was okay" and for me to change my mind. He might as well have said, "I can find others to help you do your job better." Because our faculty is a united front, we were able to use this situation to provide several important lessons in professionalism. First, your words must be trustworthy. When you do not honor your commitments, you threaten your overall dependability. Second, as described in the introduction, your actions affect more than just you. Having dishonored the agreement would have reflected poorly on the program and could harm the likelihood of other students securing a placement at that site. Third, there was a missed opportunity for the student to build more acceptance around disappointment, which is an indisputable inevitability in life.

CHAPTER 14

Dealing with Problematic Faculty

The previous chapter discussed the ways difficult faculty
test our professional composure while also offering us
opportunities to grow. Your skills in managing your professional deportment with such challenging individuals will
benefit your ultimate preparation. Consider it practice.

In this chapter, we need to differentiate difficult faculty
from problematic faculty. The line between them can sometimes be fine and difficult to draw. Just because you believe
a professor is inept, unlikeable, or overly strict does not
mean that they fall into the category of problematic. But
what about strict behavior that borders on abusive? Is it okay
that a professor calls you names, comments on your appearance, or asks you to house-sit while they are on vacation? Is
it okay for a professor to enlist a student's help in conducting
research unethically?

Students should never feel as though they have to put up
with intimidation, abuse, discrimination, sexual harassment,
retaliation, exploitation, or unethical or illegal conduct. You
should not tolerate circumstances that may be unhealthy or

harmful to you. These behaviors are incongruent with a productive learning climate and will inhibit your development and success. And they conflict with your rights as a student.

So how do you know when a faculty crosses the line and violates one of your rights? A simple test is to do a self-assessment of harm: Is there an actual or reasonable threat to your emotional, physical, or social well-being?

Is There a Threat to My Well-Being?

Social: *Does the professor's words or action harm or threaten my social standing or professional reputation? Is it congruent with the learning objectives under which I have accepted instruction?*

Emotional: *Does the professor's words or action make me feel ashamed, humiliated, isolated, or anxious?*

Physical: *Does the professor's words or action make me feel physically vulnerable?*

Consultation

If you believe you are in a situation where there is a threat to your well-being, do not rely on the advice in this book alone. Seek consultation and get more information about your avenues of redress. Unique situations often require unique responses, and persons more familiar with your faculty and university may have useful suggestions for moving forward. Always remember that you have the final decision on if and how you move forward; do not allow yourself to feel pressured by others to file a complaint if you do not want to. At the same time, do not disempower yourself just because confronting the situation seems scary.

Keep in mind that consultation excludes any kind of investigative actions, which would typically begin when you initiate an avenue of redress. This means that your consultant is only hearing your side of the story. Sources to consider for consultation include the following:

- Advisors and mentors whom you trust, including those who may be at different institutions.

- A university ombudsman is able to provide you with information about university policies and procedures. They can answer your questions and give you advice on how to navigate certain processes at the university level. Please note that they are not necessarily advocates and will not typically take your side on issues that you bring forward.

- If you are registered with a licensing board or have membership in a professional organization, it may have an ethics committee that is available for consultation. Such committees are most useful for situations where you want to compare the professor's behavior with the accepted standards of conduct outlined in the ethical codes. Licensing boards will also be able to advise you on the legality of your professor's actions and whether or not they fall within the scope of behavior defined and sanctioned by their license.

Redress

Many levels of redress are available, and each involves different numbers of stakeholders. In almost all cases, the level should match the severity of the offense and, when possible, should be initiated at the lowest levels first. In addition to matching the method to the situation, your level of response will depend on a number of factors, including the following:

1. The degree to which the issue negatively affects your functioning and development. Use the test to determine if there is a threat to your well-being and consult with others about how the issue affects you in both the short and long term.

2. The degree to which you can demonstrate an adverse impact on your social, emotional, or physical well-being.

3. The degree to which you are willing to participate in due process proceedings (some of which may be obligatory).

4. The amount of privacy you prefer. Higher levels of redress are likely to attract more attention.

Several other factors may apply, but they are specific to the avenues chosen. Please note that the objective of this chapter is to advise students on strategies for stopping behavior that is harming their education and development. That objective does not include retaliating, seeking justice, or securing compensation for damages. Those personal choices fall outside the topic of this book and should be made with appropriate legal counsel. For these reasons, the options discussed here typically exist within the university and not outside of it. To stop harmful behaviors, the following list provides some intervention options.

- *Informal resolution.* Informal resolution is the lowest level of intervention and involves addressing the complaint directly with the professor. In some situations, before other avenues of redress become available, it may be required that the person first be made aware that their behaviors are unwanted. This advanced professional skill requires you to actively manage discomfort while communicating directly and effectively. If the situation seems too intense or intimidating, or if you are concerned about how the professor will react, you may have opportunities to enlist a third party who can help mediate the discussion. Be aware that third parties in these situations should never be used to corner or outnumber the professor.

- *The program's due process procedures.* Each program should have its own due process procedures outlined either in the course catalog or in their student handbook. These procedures outline the steps you can take to file a grievance, how the grievance will be reviewed, and the opportunities for appeal. If the issue is particularly egregious, you may use this avenue and forego attempting an informal resolution. The process typically begins with a grievance submitted to the program director or department chair. If the complaint involves the director or chair, you should be able to submit the grievance to the next level (such as the dean).

- *Title IX Coordinator.* For issues of sexual harassment or sexual assault, please contact your Title IX coordinator to discuss the problem. Please note that the coordinator may be required by law to take certain actions without your consent.

- *Disability services.* If the issue involves the neglect of a disability accommodation, the disability office can assist you with options and advice for moving forward.

Handling Yourself During Due Process

Filing a grievance is a right that you have as a student. It is part of the checks and balances that ensure your protection against unfairness and mistreatment. Some students may feel uneasy filing a grievance because they fear it will create negative feelings among the faculty or somehow result in retaliation, subtle or otherwise. Sometimes students avoid using grievances because they do not want to be perceived as querulous. Maintaining your professional deportment during this process minimizes the chances that your actions will be seen as anything other than an honest clarification of your educational rights. Following are a few ways to showcase your professionalism when filing a grievance:

- *Be truthful.* Focus on describing behaviors that you have observed in the context of your complaint. Simply describe what happened with as little emotional charge as possible. Avoid using any judgments, labels, and character traits to describe the alleged perpetrator.

- *Link the issue to an inconsistency with policy or training objectives.* Your complaint has the most traction when you can demonstrate that it is inconsistent with what was promised to you as a student. For example, a professor who berates students is not creating an atmosphere conducive to learning, which is a commitment commonly found in the university's statement on Student Rights and Responsibilities.

- *Isolate the problem.* Discuss only the issue and its personal impact on you. Avoid the temptation to generalize the problem by making broad, sweeping judgments about the program. Do not wrap all of your other gripes about the program into your grievance.

- *Do not skip steps.* Avoid the temptation to skip steps in the due process by going over heads and appealing to higher officials first. Some students become so disgruntled that they fire off angry letters directly to the provost or university president. This is never appropriate, and all that happens is that the student gets redirected to the program and the due process procedures.

- *Take responsibility where you have it.* If there was something that you could have either done or not done to help or prevent the situation, now is the time to mention it. For example, certain unethical behaviors begin mildly and progressively worsen over time, so intervening earlier can sometimes prevent the escalation. Protecting both yourself and the other person is also protecting the profession.

- *Do not use a grievance to retaliate.* It does not make sense to lie in wait for a professor you dislike to slip up so that you can pounce on them with a grievance.

- *Do not abuse the grievance system.* Using the system repeatedly or in ways other than which it is intended may create patterns that faculty find concerning.

- *Be gracious with outcomes.* A professional consensus is a common way to determine whether something should have or should not have occurred when the situation is specific, unique, or unprecedented. Each time someone provides another supportive opinion, either in the initial grievance or in subsequent appeals, the number of people contributing to that consensus increases. If the outcome is unsatisfactory to you and each appeal renders the same opinion, the chances of systemic unfairness against you become increasingly unlikely. At this point, the earlier discussion about defensiveness may be useful as a quick self-assessment. Is your redress really about wanting to avoid something? Is there an important lesson here for you?

CHAPTER 15

Self-Care

Why is there a chapter on self-care in a book about professional etiquette? Self-care relates directly to a very important aspect of professionalism: knowing your limits. Professionals who do not know their limits will extend themselves beyond their own usefulness, become a liability to their clients, and travel down a path to "burnout." When caring about your work feels like a waste of energy, when you feel you are just spinning your wheels, and when even little tasks become overwhelming, you are experiencing some of the symptoms of burnout. You might also feel as though your work has no impact and is meaningless. Or you may feel disengaged, numb, or drained.

In psychotherapy, we say, "you can't pour from an empty pitcher." That is, we cannot give our best care and attention to our clients when we are physically, mentally, or emotionally depleted. The same goes for any other profession: When you begin to experience apathy, pessimism, or cynicism, you are more likely to begin caring less about the quality of your work. Knowing when you are getting close to this point is extremely important in not only preserving your well-being but also protecting the public that you serve. Caring for your clients necessarily means caring for yourself.

This issue is so important for graduate students that I make it a point to ask about it in every admissions interview. The demands of graduate school are extremely high. Graduate school will challenge you intellectually because you will find the academic rigor more intense. It will challenge you socially because the time required for reading, writing, and completing projects will supplant the time you would have used to spend with your family and friends. It will challenge you physically as your intense schedule will change your usual eating, sleeping, and exercise routines. It will challenge you financially because most graduate programs are expensive. Lastly, it will challenge you emotionally as you begin practicing the enormous responsibilities that come with your profession, whether it is caring for patients, managing workers, or navigating complex and confusing social structures.

The first step in developing effective self-care is to increase your awareness of your own symptoms of stress or burnout. Everyone experiences it differently. How will you know that you are moving toward an ineffective place? See the list of examples given here and spend some time thinking about which are most likely to happen to you during times of heightened stress. These are your warning signs:

- *Physical Sensations*: low energy, fatigue, headaches, nausea, teeth clenching, muscle tension

- *Emotional Reactions*: feeling over-whelmed, irritability, moodiness, sadness, fearfulness, anxiety

- *Thoughts and Mental Life*: racing thoughts, worry, poor memory, difficulty focusing, pessimism, doubt

- *Behavioral Signs*: quick to react, fidgety, restless, slow moving or moping, sighing heavily, pacing

When the stress becomes chronic or perpetual, the following behavioral symptoms may begin:

Acting Out	Acting In
• Labeling, disparaging, or judging others • Not caring about the quality of your work • Overscheduling or overworking yourself • Complaining • Neglecting required duties (such as homework assignments) • Becoming short, impatient, or irritable with others • Becoming forgetful • Missing or skipping appointments or other meetings; coming late, leaving early • Excessive cynicism and sarcasm • Procrastinating	• Withdrawing from your peers • Withdrawing from friends and family • Daydreaming in class, practicum, or supervision • Questioning your fitness for the field or lamenting the loss of other career opportunities • Compartmentalizing your struggles or minimizing their impact • Dropping out of your regular activities • Self-medicating • Self-doubt

As you reflect on these examples, do you think you are an "acting out" or "acting in" kind of person? How might burnout, as expressed in these behaviors, negatively affect your professional reputation?

Faculty often see their academic programs as microcosmic laboratories of the larger society. How you handle the challenges of graduate school will be an indicator of how you handle the challenges of the profession after you graduate. For this reason, some programs deliberately escalate stress to see how you will react. If the stress of graduate school makes you forgetful or miss appointments, there is no reason for the faculty to believe that this will be different when you are stressed as a professional. There is no, "I'll be better later when it matters." If difficult faculty push you into becoming passive-aggressive, difficult bosses will do the same. Being aware of and effectively managing your stress will preempt and mitigate these kinds of unprofessional reactions. Graduate school is the place to begin developing your awareness of stress.

Following sufficient work on awareness, the next step is to have a self-care plan in place that effectively manages that stress. It is important to develop self-care practices before you get to the point of burning out; if you have these activities preemptively integrated into your schedule, when you become stressed you will have ready access to your resources. If you do not have them in place at the time things get real, then you will just have extra work to do on top of feeling stressed out.

A healthy diet, exercise, creative endeavors, hobbies, music, meditation, and time with friends and family are among the activities that can replenish your personal resources. Effective self-care has several characteristics and includes the following:

- *Consistency*: Your self-care should be built into a routine with a specific time set aside for it.

- *Involvement of another person, to ensure accountability*: Does a friend or loved one know about your self-care plan? Do they tell you to stop working when you are supposed to be playing?

- *Activities that span several life areas*: Your plan should include activities that satisfy you socially, emotionally, spiritually, physically, and mentally.

Mindfulness

It is not uncommon for students to say that they engaged in a self-care activity but did not find it refreshing. They may say that they spent the afternoon at the beach but worried the entire time about a paper that was due. In other words, their body was at the beach, but their mind was not. This does not count as self-care.

Full immersion in your self-care takes practice and can be enhanced with mindfulness. Mindfulness is training your attention, recognizing when you are being taken away by your thoughts, and coming back to the present moment. It means being where you are when you are. Thoughts and worries do not need to be changed, defeated, or driven away for us to be present; we just need to practice letting go so that we regain control of how we direct our attention. We can do this when we see thoughts for what they are: just thoughts.

Mindfulness has proven benefits for many aspects of life, including reduced stress and emotional reactivity, better sleep, improved memory and focus, broader perspective, and greater cognitive flexibility. I highly recommend considering it as part of your self-care routine.

Values

While engaging in activities that bring us pleasure is helpful for our self-care, it is equally helpful to commit to actions that bring us purpose and meaning. Your values clarify what is important in your life. They answer the question, "What do you want your life to be about?"

Many people find values in relationships, worship, health, citizenship, hobbies, and work, and they are often best stated with an adjective that describes a desired quality. For example, someone may value being a "caring friend," or a "strong advocate for the underserved." Values are directions and not destinations; we always have opportunities to move ourselves in directions that are important to us.

An exercise that can help you clarify your values is to write a draft of your own obituary. It may sound morbid but take some time to seriously contemplate what you would want written to the world about your life. You are likely to see personal characteristics that you want to be remembered by emerge in your writing. Those are values.

Once you have values defined, the next step is to build a list of activities that demonstrate movement towards those values. For example, to the person in the previous paragraph that said they value being a caring friend, they may live out that value by phoning friends periodically to check in on them, sending cards, helping them with problems, random acts of kindness, and making time to have lunch together. The meaning inherent in being a caring friend is *created* through these small actions. We have opportunities every day to make these kinds of choices, to spend small amounts of time engaged in something important to us. We can even do them when we are feeling stressed out.

Creating meaning by living a valued life directly combats the cynicism, helplessness, and apathy that are commonly experienced in burnout. Because values are intrinsically motivating, they provide sources of energy from which we can draw to actualize the best versions of our selves. They are reasons for carrying on.

Concluding Thoughts

I hope that any concerns created by reading this book do not overshadow the growth potential that awaits you in graduate school. Academia is a deeply personal pursuit, and through it you are likely to build formative relationships that alter your social trajectory, gain access to cutting-edge approaches, and find mentors who truly care about you as a person. You will encounter opportunities to practice alongside the current movers and shakers, learn from the "old guard," and witness the emergence of innovation. You may experience radical shifts in your worldview, learn skillful means in walking the world, and find a deepening sense of purpose.

Professionalism is also about all of these things. Your profession was built before you and is carried through time by those who have adopted it as part of their identity. To build a professional identity means that you, too, accept the responsibility and commitment that your profession has promised to society. It is a noble undertaking, one that requires ongoing personal growth and selfless dedication. Your willingness to honestly examine these principles within yourself is a testament to your value as a true professional.

ABOUT THE AUTHOR

Psychologist and associate professor Ryan Sharma has been mentoring students through higher education for over 14 years, teaching classes in professionalism, consultation, and clinical supervision. In his role as the director of clinical training at California Lutheran University, he helps students develop their professional identity so that they can be successful working alongside seasoned clinicians. When he is not teaching or treating anxiety in his private practice, he is either woodworking or spending time with his wife and three children.

If you found this book useful, please leave a review.